Choose Life

Poetry, Prose, and Photography

Reflecting the Life Philosophy of
the Artist's 100-year-old Father, Ken Ogren

Jan Ögren

Storyteller, Photographer, and Psychotherapist

ISBN-13: 978-0692816271
ISBN-10: 0692816275

First Printing, 2017
Updated Version, 2021

Photography by Jan Ögren

www.JanOgren.net
Published by Namen Press
NamenPress@gmail.com

Namen Press

OTHER BOOKS BY JAN ÖGREN

Dividing Worlds
Namen Press, 2011

Mundos em Divisao: Uma Parabola Para Nossos Tempos
Barany Publisher, 2014
Sao Paulo, Brazil

Dragon Magic: Amazing Fables for All Ages
Namen Press, 2015

Ken Ogren on the trail to Vernal Falls with a view of upper Yosemite Falls.
Yosemite, California. March, 2017

Dedication

To my father, Ken Ogren.

As a child growing up in Minnesota, my father had rheumatic fever three winters in a row. His parents carefully nurtured him through each episode, but the doctors told him not to expect to live past 40 years old. When he was 63 years old, he suffered from a debilitating major depression. My mother, Marjorie, helped him navigate a year and a half of medical dead ends, until finally discovering the medication that restored his equilibrium. In 2006, Marjorie was thrown into a medication-induced depression that she never fully recovered from. He was her devoted primary caregiver until her death in 2013, two weeks after they celebrated their 64th anniversary.

Through all these and more experiences, my dad learned to cherish and enjoy life. He is still teaching me to take risks, and challenging me to be fully myself. Learning to snorkel for the first time at age 87, hiking in the Rocky Mountains at age 95, and giving his first Sunday service at a Unitarian Universalist congregation at age 97, he demonstrates his willingness to explore and experience life to its fullest.

At 100 years old, he saw his life's purpose as encouraging people to look forward to growing older, to try something new, to be positive, to work to build a better world, and to exercise daily.

To help create this book, my father chose which of my poems and photographs best represent his philosophy of life.

I'm honored to dedicate this book to Ken Ogren.

CONTENTS

I Choose Life

≈✺≈

II Death and Life

≈✺≈

III Eternal

≈✺≈

IV Relationships

≈✿≈

V Adventure

≈✿≈

VI Self-Reflections

≈✿≈

Acknowledgments

This book has been inspired by people, nature, spirits, and my own imagination. I am grateful to all who have helped me in the journey to share these poems, prose, and photography.

Many of the poems in this book were written for my mother toward the end of her life. She had difficulty maintaining a positive outlook, but somehow my poems seemed to reach her. They encouraged her to remember the joy she always had for life. She loved my poems and I loved sharing them with her.

Writing poems is only half the process. They come alive in the presence of a reader, so I am incredibly grateful to those who gave me feedback: Andrea Selieta Williamson, Cat Capitani, Dale Jenkins, Dean Watson, Judith Goleman, Kate Sorensen, Ken Ogren, Kitty Wells, Lisa Beytia, Sheridan Gold, Dr. Venus Maher, Vickie Rodriguez, and Shelley Stewart, MSW.

Thanks to Redwood Writers (branch of California Writers Club) and to all who have encouraged me, and especially to Jeane Slone and Sher Gamard.

Special thanks to my white cat, Esprit, for being a model for many of the photographs, and for all the purring and lap-time he performed while trying to distract me from writing. And to my new cat, Star, who together with Esprit, were so annoyingly intelligent that they gave me the most popular sentence I ever wrote (see my bio on the back cover).

And finally, thanks to Cris Wanzer of Book and Manuscript Services for seeing the book as I envisioned it and weaving the poems and photography so perfectly.

Foreword

Everyone Does It*

Jan Ögren

My father did not die of aspiration pneumonia. That's what his death certificate states, but it's not true. They wouldn't allow me to write in the real reason. A death certificate requires a cause of death. A person isn't permitted to just die. There must be something to blame, something that goes wrong as if death is a mistake. But death happens to everyone. My dad knew that. That's why he planned his one-hundredth birthday as a memorial service for himself.

≈⁂≈

December third, 2018 was his one-hundredth birthday. What a celebration it was! A week full of festivities. Hiking a mile in the redwoods with his Swedish cousins. Going to San Francisco and picking up the children of life-long friends and then taking them around Golden Gate Park. A five-course French dinner for 21 people. And then on his actual birthday a celebration in the style of a Unitarian Universalist memorial service.

My dad stood behind the podium, in his pink dress shirt and bollo tie, at the beginning of his 100th birthday celebration, looking out at the crowd of 130 people and said, "This is my memorial service, and I am here! Too often I've been at memorial services and the person being honored isn't there. That doesn't seem right. So I'm here for mine." He smiled and looked around as people cheered him. He raised his arms high above his head, clasping his hands as though he'd just won a gold medal.

"Thank you for coming. To light the chalice for my service, I'm going to read a poem called 'Choose Life.' Three years ago my daughter told me she wanted to dedicate her next book to me, and what would I like? Right away I said I want a book of your poetry and photography. I got to pick out all my favorite poems and this one is the title poem from the book *Choose Life*."

He read the poem, as I lit the chalice. Then my dad continued, "People ask me how did I do it? How is that I'm 100 years old and happy? Well, I'm going to tell you my five philosophies." He reached up and tapped his forehead. "Think positively. Try something new. Look forward to growing older. Yes, I did say look forward to growing older! Work to build a better world for all. And exercise daily, or almost daily." He added the last with a smile. Even though he did exercise every day, he didn't want to discourage anyone if they didn't do it daily.

The minister said it was the most joyful memorial service he'd ever performed. It was also the easiest because my dad wrote out the script for him; after all, he did like to be in control. The minister shared how my father was raised Swedish Methodist on a small farm in Minnesota. He left that faith when he went to the University of Minnesota. It was too confining for him, just like living on a farm was not the life he wanted. He was an explorer. He wanted to figure out life for himself, not be told what to believe or what to do every day.

When my dad discovered Unitarian Universalism he knew he'd found a spiritual home. Here was a religion that allowed him to be an atheist, and later an agnostic. He lived without a belief or a concept of what would happen after death and for him, it was the big unknown.

We showed pictures of him, we sang songs and people got up and talked about him, just like they'd do at a memorial service. Only he got to be there for all of it. At the end my dad came back up to do the closing words. "I started my service with the poem 'Choose Life,'" he said. "Now I'm going to end with two poems about death. The first one is called. 'I Plan to Die.' I've always been annoyed when people say 'if I die' as though it's an option. It's not. Everyone will die. The second poem is called, 'Pack Love' about how all you need for your last journey is love." He read the two poems and then everyone sang happy birthday to him. The pianist, who was a professional jazz musician, played a boogie-woogie improve on happy birthday and my dad and I danced on stage, as the audience sprang to their feet and cheered him.

Eighteen days after his birthday Dad decided to go on hospice. He didn't want someone calling an ambulance and sending him to the hospital, as he got ready to die. There was an obstacle to his qualifying for hospice though, he had no terminal diagnosis. He was in good health. But since he was 100 years old the nurse said, "We'll admit you, then reevaluate you in three months."

After filling out all the paperwork he turned to me and asked, "Do we still have time to go to that Irish Christmas show tonight?"

"Sure Dad," I said, "why not go out and celebrate going on hospice." It was a good way to avoid thinking that he was planning to die. The poem he read at his memorial, 'I Plan to Die,' begins: "I plan to die. Not next Thursday and not before the holidays." And he did that. He lived through Christmas and New Year's so that he wouldn't leave us with his death over the holidays. The poem ends with the line: "All my life, I have planned, as my final act - to die." And that's what he did on January fifth, two weeks after entering hospice.

I wish I'd asked him more about how he knew he was going to die. Every time I tried, I got so choked up with tears it was hard to talk, and then we'd just look at each other and we knew. We knew the time was coming and he wanted to die naturally, in good health.

He didn't die of any cause or reason. He died because he knew how to let go. He'd been practicing it for years. Letting go of friends, letting go of his much-beloved wife, letting go of being able to travel long distances, letting go of being able to cross-country ski and climb mountains.

People asked me if there would be a memorial service, but I said, "No, we had it, he planned it, and he was there." We did have a brief service with the minister and forty people when we put his ashes in the memorial garden at the church. My mother died in 2013, just after their sixty-fourth anniversary. Her ashes were placed in the memorial garden and everytime I took my dad to church we paused at the garden. He would point to where her ashes were and say, "someday that's where I'll be, right next to her." His final words, that the minister read were, "I enjoy life. Each step along the way has given me new experiences. I don't look back at the past with regrets or nostalgia. Every year has been the best yet."

* Previously published in *California Writers Club Literary Review 2020* and *Sunset Sunrise:: A Collection of Endings and Beginnings*, Redwood Writers 2020 Anthology.

I
CHOOSE LIFE

Choose Life

Go ahead, Choose Life.

No — not fifteen minutes of fame,
the untouchable stash of money in the vault, or
the unknown gorgeous person on your arm.

Life — as in
bruised knees,
apple blossoms,
and thunderstorms.

Choose life —
not perfection, but exploration.
Not control, but curiosity.

Look at life —
turn the mirror around,
stop reflecting others, and witness your own image.

The world may not be what you expected —
so you don't have to be what society expects.

Listen to life.
Apple blossoms want you here.
Thunderstorms want you here.
Life wants you,
   and if you don't know that now,
     — wait, and you will.

So go ahead.
   Choose Life.

GRUMBLING

I want to grumble,
just grumble.
"At what?" you ask.
At everything, anything.

I want to kick a stone down the street
over and over again,
until my nice, new black shoes are scuffed
and I can grumble at the stone that caused it.

I want to grumble,
like a thunderstorm
closing in on the plains.
I want to throw my rain down on corn shoots
and twisted trees and hatless heads.

I want to grumble,
like a herd of horses
throwing mud up as we charge across the prairie,
rearing and snorting, heads high, tails outstretched.

"Done yet?" you ask.
No.
No, I am not finished yet.

I still want to grumble.
"Why?" you ask.

Well, I'm good at it.
That's what my mother says.
My teachers all think I do it the best.
Someone needs to grumble.
There's not much more to grumble about so
I think I'll rage now.

I want to roll boulders
down a mountainside.
And rage at the dust
that gets thrown back in my eyes.

I want to rage like lightning,
challenging the genteel clouds for the sky.
I want to burst forth with the light,
startling the jays, the joggers, and the riverbanks.

I want to rage like a stampede of elephants.
Flowing over the earth,
trumpeting and bellowing
and calling ourselves home.

And now — I think I'll cry.
Like a songbird after a storm.
I'll cry like a mother cat whose kittens
have wandered off.
I'll cry like me, when I am tired
and no one has fixed me dinner.

And then maybe I'll rest,
and wait,
until I erupt again.

Paradoxes of Being

I have to be me.

But who am I?

A reflection
of you?
of my parents?
of society?
of what?

Can someone help me to be me,
without me becoming them?

When is being me merely a reaction to you
and not me at all?

If I am walking alone in the woods and no one hears me — do I exist?

Maybe I only exist as I relate to
evergreens, hawks, and you.
Maybe I am one piece of a giant jigsaw puzzle.

What if my contours and shades
can only be perceived
when aligned with the whole?

Maybe this being a totally unique me
in the absence of others is a mistake,
a myth,
a miscalculation
where I forget that I need to add
you, rivers and towns
to equal me.

Maybe I should try to remember all the others,
not get so focused on who I am,
that I forget I don't exist without you.

Then we can all be united
so the picture will be all-embracing
and we won't lose pieces or species.
        No big ME's taking up all the room.

After all,
mosaics are most magnificent
the smaller the individual pieces are.

THE GIFT OF HEALTH

I used to think we took care of ourselves
for ourselves.
I used to think what I did affected only me.
      If I came in late,
       drank too much,
well... *"it's my life, isn't it?"*

Then I walk into the hospital room
      and see you
encircled by tubes, a wailing machine for breath,
      and a table of jumbled-up medication bottles.

And I know,
life is not solitary.

"It's my life. I can do what I want,"
      you declare,
when you have enough strength to demand a cigarette.

No. No, I think silently.
You owe it to those who love you.

Damn it, you could have chosen health.
Now, you lie there
all tubes and tattered life
coming undone in a white-washed hospital room.

We didn't have to be here now.
You're too young,
      and it's too soon,
        and it's all wrong.

My protests go unheard,
        unheeded.
And I am left washing your cold body.
Screaming,
"You had no right to belittle my love with cigarettes
and bad food."

After the memorial service,
I'm giving up the bottle and fast driving.
I'll even start paying attention to what I eat.
        I want to give my loved ones
                the gift of my own health.

THE COURAGE OF MEDIOCRITY

Bravo for those who finish in the middle.
Three cheers for the "losers"!

Our society recognizes gold medals, Oscars, Nobel prizes, best-sellers, and other "bests." But what if a person's *best* is not *the best?* With the increases in population, communication, and transportation the top one hundredth of a percent of life: the thinkers, scientists, artists, writers, explorers, athletes, and performers that are the best of the best are paraded before us daily.

What happens to the people who give their heart and soul to a contest and then are labeled "losers" by society, so that one person can claim the title "winner"? How do we answer a child, or adult, who asks: "Why try, if I know I can't win?" "Why run a race if I know I will be in the middle?" Why should we make an attempt if our efforts will only be mediocre? That is such a terrible judgment. Most people would prefer to be called many other names than mediocre. I had to look up the word in a dictionary just to verify that it really does mean average or ordinary, and not worthless or disdainful.

Mediocre, average, ordinary is where, by definition, the majority of people reside when life is based on comparisons. In competitions and testing, the middle area is always the largest section. Yet we tend to focus on the extreme top end.

Long ago when I was in high school, I remember showing up in that unique place for the college entrance exams. I scored in the 99.99 percentile in math. I wondered then about the people scoring 80%, 50%, or 30%. There had to be so many people in those other sections for me to be in the top .01%. It took no great courage for me to score that high, I was a natural math intuitive. In English I scored much lower, showing up in the average range, mediocre. I have found it takes more courage for me to be an ordinary writer than it ever did for me to be exceptional in math. If I had wanted to go for being the best, I should have focused on numbers, yet my love is for words. Here, I need all the strength I can muster, because if I focus on writing perfectly or being the best, I will stop loving what I write. I will be in danger of asking myself the deadly question, "Why write, if I can't guarantee it will be a best seller?"

Looking over the bookshelves, seeing all the writers and books out there, I know I just need to be there. Not the best, just me. If I write a mediocre book then it will exist. People will be able to read and enjoy it. If I wait until I can be assured I will write the next best seller, it will stay forever on my laptop or in my mind, buried beneath judgments and fears.

I wonder: what would it be like if our society measured a person's worth by internal satisfaction, rather than external comparisons? What if in place of beauty contests we had self-esteem or happiness contests? What if the winner of the race was not the first person, but the one who crossed the finish line with the biggest smile? What if people were encouraged to follow what they loved, not what they were "good" at? Or what if we just stopped having competitions completely and trusted that children and adults would naturally want to explore their talents with no need for pressure or coercion?

Until the world does change, I'll continue to cheer for all those that do *their* best, and are not *the* best. Bravo for the people in the middle and at the end. The ones who run the race, because they know it is their race to run, and they are brave enough to participate in life.

CHANCE

Drive fast, faster, faster!
Push the pedal, grip the wheel,
look for an opening,
a chance to pass.

Winding, two-lane road,
stuck behind tourists,
looking at cows
and enormous oak trees.

Finally, they signal,
cautiously turning by the meadow.
At last! Here's my chance.
Clear acceleration to the next blind turn.

Only ten minutes before my meeting.
Please, no trucks, no tourists, and no lost souls
looking, looking,
and driving slow.

Red lights ahead.
Red fire engine, ambulance, police cars.
I stop.
No other choice.

I watch the ambulance go by,
carrying you off,
transporting you straight into uncertainty.
Had you been rushing toward a meeting too?

I'm going nowhere now.
I turn off the engine.
I will be late.

Nothing I can do.

Cars bunch up behind me.
I'm in a dead zone,
no reception, no messages.
I turn off the cell phone.

The tow truck drags away the twisted remnants of your car.
No more meetings for you — for a while.
Your calendar emptied
— in a single second.

II
DEATH AND LIFE

Planning to Die

I plan to die.

Not next Thursday.
Probably not before the holidays.

But some day,
some year.

I do plan to die.

It is not an "if."
And I will not simply "pass away," "kick the bucket,"
or "take a long trip."
I certainly don't want to be "lost."
I won't even agree to "expire."
I am going to die.

I'm sorry if it disturbs you,
— that I don't pretend I will live forever,
but I don't want death sneaking up —
surprising me and my friends.

I want everyone to know that I do intend to die.
It won't be a mistake — or a failure,
all my life, I have planned,
as my final act — to die.

Remember to Pack Love

Remember to care for the part of you that continues on
— after this life.
It's here now, hiding inside.
More than a breath,
more than a pulse.

The moment people shed their skins,
you know —
there is more missing in those cold corpses
than just a smile.
Someone was there.
Where they have gone is nonphysical
    — so enjoy the touch of your lover's hand.
Savor the sweetness of raspberries in spring.

But don't forget that part of you that will continue on
— past life.
Help it to prepare for its journey.
Don't bother packing the business suits
and fancy clothes,
no need for extra underwear, or even a toothbrush.
There's nothing you have struggled to buy
that it will want.
But what should you pack for it?
Perhaps some love, self-awareness, memories?

You could heed the advice
of those who have gone before.
It's always the same:
*"Pack lighter — I took too much.
Just yourself — is all you need."*

So unpack those fears and shoulds.
Quit obsessing about what you don't have,
Let go of what you haven't done yet.

You'll be fine.
Love more, fear less
and you'll be perfectly prepared
for death.

STRAWBERRY

First it was a dream.
Then a blossom on a vine
connected to soil, raindrops, and sun.

My fingers knew it as solid,
a Braille of seeds
in heart-shaped wonder.

In my mouth, pure liquid
exploding on my tongue,
then it was gone.

Blood-red fingers
a passing tribute
to what is now me.

LOOKING FOR DEATH IN THE FOREST

"Amen,"
everyone says, as the memorial service ends.
I drive away, images of my friend trailing behind me.
Why, Death, why?
Why did she have to die?
No reply.

I turn left, away from town.
I can't go home yet.
I need to know —
Why?

Tears blur my vision.
I pull off the road
and enter shadows.
Trees tower over me
as I stumble into a forest.

Is there an answer for me here?

A fallen tree beckons.
I kneel beside it.
Certain I have found Death,
I pound my fists against its bark.
Why, Death?
Why did you take my friend?
No reply.

I look at where my questions are dented
into the toppled giant.
I almost smashed a young shoot,
a tiny version of the life that had fallen.

24

Letting my vision glide
over the slumbering
log,
I now see dozens of
small growths.
No wonder Death is
not answering me.
This is not true death.

I continue my search.
I approach a jagged
stump, lightning
scarred.
I examine it minutely.
No new growth, no
green shoots.
Not even a vine
twisting around this
blackened hulk.
Surely this is Death.
*"I have found you,
NOW!"* I shout.
"NOW, Now, now," the wind
echoes back.

The former tree quivers.
I fear it will collapse.
Stepping back, I see its future.
Bit by bit falling in on itself,
drifting to the forest floor.

Frustrated, I try to shake off the vision.
I want my answer!
But instead I see
a mound of life,
that used to be a stump,
used to be a jagged scar,
used to be a living tree.
Now I see it becoming vines and sprouts,
ferns and potential.

I leave the woods.
Death will not answer me here.
Setting my car toward home,
I think of my friend.
She loved forests and gardens.

I'm home.
Still enough glow in the sky
to allow me to be outside.

The frost was cruel this winter.
One of my favorite azalea bushes died.
I kneel by it,
reaching down to push away the debris at the base.
I want a good grip so I can pull it up cleanly,
replace it quickly.

My hand brushes against something soft.
Peering closer, I see a shoot,
just next to the dead trunk, and all alone.
I check every branch.
No green, no buds, no attempts at buds.
Only this small speck of growth.

It had been a sizable bush, central in my garden.
This green, so small, not even a leaf yet,
will need years to fill the void.

I stop searching for Death and listen to Life.
I'm still here. I'm still here, it whispers.
I return the mulch around the remains of the old bush,
gently covering the shoot.
I'll let it come out,
when it is ready.

Dying Without Her

"I am NOT going to die," she proclaimed.
>   —   Not going to die?
> Her body is throbbing
> with disease and agony.

"I am NOT ill," she declared.
>   —   Not ill?
> Her body is shaking
> with anguish and pain.

"I WILL get better," she commanded.
>   —   Ah, what assurance!
> knowing her future,
> predicting and directing it
> like a general from her hospital bed.

"I am NOT dying," she insisted.
> So finally,
> disheartened,
> ignored,
> her body had to die without her.

> No chance for goodbyes,
> celebrations,
> or love.

"I am NOT dying," echoed off the walls
    at the memorial service.
    Was challenged by the tears
    cascading down her children's cheeks.

    Her body had to die without her.
    It couldn't wait
    for her to remember
    to come home.

III
Eternal

GOD

God.
Good God, God
What do I do with you?
You come with so much baggage.

Thousands of years of projections, anthropomorphizing,
judgments, proclamations, killings, burnings,
bounty, beauty, and blessings.

I wish we could both start fresh.
Date, as though we had just met
so I could get to know you without all your past:
your history.

But no, not you God.
You've had a relationship with everyone.
There's no one you're not passionately married to,
or irreconcilably divorced from.

Sometimes I just want to walk out
and never speak your name again.

But if I left, what would happen to you, God?
You keep letting others decide what and who you are.
Don't you have any pride?
For God's sake, God, have some backbone.
Stand up. Stop the wars. Shake off all the prejudice.
Don't just sit there.

Oh God,
Maybe if you could just change your name.
Or even a different language might help.

Dieu, Dios, Deo.
Ah, now we're getting somewhere.
They float off the tongue.
Twist in the air as a cloud, taking on different shapes.

But God,
you just sit there.
Heavy, with piles of baggage all around.
God — you are such a noun.

You need to be a verb.
I want to go god-ing.
Then I could say: "I god-ed the universe this morning as the sun rose."
And when I'm feeling miserable,
my friends could touch me in my pain
and god me.

If you won't agree to be a verb,
how about at least an adjective?
Then I could refer to the god-ish colored rose.
Or the god-ness of my love making.

But you wouldn't do as an adverb.
To act god-ly. Too judgmental.
Here comes the baggage again.

I think I like you best as a verb.

Maybe we can try god-ing together?
And I won't abandon you to all the prejudices;
won't let them use you for war anymore.
I won't even change your name.
I'll just go about god-ing the world,
the best I can.

Dancing Oak

Grand, growing Oak,
dancing in the field.
What soft decades of harmonies
are you listening to?

You let me glimpse your strong, solid form,
and in that instant, I see you dance.
Each precise movement, every twist and sway
executed by decades and balanced by days.

Your naked body holding each pose —
limbs, branches, twigs
bending, stretching, curving
enough to make a yogi envious.

Each gesture reminds me of a million winds
blowing through your field,
the eternalness of sunshine
pulling you into the sky.

And what triumph of dances
is happening underground?
If I could but see your other half —
roots twined and braided into earthly hair.

What would it be like to grow my shape?
To stand still in a field,
and move by fractions, not miles.
To dance to the rhythms of the earth?

To move an inch a year,
dancing until the harmony is clear,
and I can show the world —
the inner music present for all to hear.

GOD AS METAPHOR

Is God beige, blue, purple or pink?
Does He, or She,
really know what we think?

Is it God All-Mighty?
Or the Mighty-All?
— as in everything —
from the sap in trees,
to the scrapes on knees.

Is God an apple, peach or pear?
And why do people care?
Arguing about the color of "His" hair,
the shade of His skin,
and what shape His eyes come in.

Ultimately
their discussions have no sway
because,
no one can debate away
interconnectedness.
Just look at
photosynthesis.

So it really doesn't matter
if you think "He" is short or tall,
because
God is a metaphor, after all.

REDWOOD

A tree passed me by the other day,
as it journeyed into the next century.
Tireless companion to eternity,
it trod on, not noticing me,
as I gazed at its fiery bark,
glowing in the rising sun.

A tree passed me by the other day.
Maybe if I had stood still a year or two
it might have greeted me.
But I didn't have the time,
I didn't create the patience,
so I'll never know
a Redwood's "Hello."

What do I Believe?

What do I believe?
Who am I?

I have to be an Agnostic,
because I don't believe —
I could hold all wisdom,
absolutely, certainly.

I must be a Pagan,
because I love nature —
listening to singing trees,
dancing, celebrating.

I'm inspired to be Jewish,
because I see myself as chosen —
living a purposeful life,
reflecting, contemplating.

I live like a Christian,
because I care for others —
helping my neighbors,
loving, sharing.

I feel like a Muslim,
because I adore peace —
praying for connection to oneness,
giving, honoring.

I eat like a Hindu,
because I honor animals —
seeking to live life with
consequences,
working, respecting.

I sit like a Buddhist,
because I try to be mindful —
freeing myself from illusions,
suffering, struggling.

I think like a Humanist,
because I like to question —
using my mind for exploring,
inquiring, analyzing.

I'm called an Atheist
because I don't believe —
in the big guy in the sky,
all-knowing, all-judging.

I worship and appreciate everything.
And because they say
that God is everything —
I guess I am a Theist too.

Who am I?
Everyone.

IV
Relationships

ONE, BY ONE, BY ONE

One, by One, by One
coming together.

Two, by Three, by Four
perhaps there's more.

They say we don't have numbers.
They say we don't matter.

Yet we keep appearing
One, by One, by One.

Now a Dozen,
Now a Thousand,
what do numbers really mean?

Isn't each of us important?
As a one? A someone?

One, by One, by One
we come,
we stand,
we make
a difference.

I Care

"I care."
>　There, I said it.

Did I cross a line?
Will you reject me?
>　Unfriend me?

We are still getting to know each other.
We call each other "friend,"
Facebook friend,
we Twitter, we text,
we've exchanged cell phone numbers and
e-mail addresses,
but I don't know the day you were born,
or if you have any siblings.

We have carefully built our friendship
>　on walls and protocols,
not wanting to intrude.
After all — we are both busy people.

Yet this feeling has grown within me
since meeting you — and now I have a name for it:
I care.

So reject me if you will
or call me old-fashioned,
but I want to let you know —
I care about you.

>　So where do we go from here?

LONELY

I'm lonely —
 I admit it.

Now, I have declared myself needy,
vulnerable,
a person to be avoided.

To gain friends I must present myself as happy,
independent,
a person who has everything,
needs nothing.

I must look as though I am entirely self-sufficient.
Then I will be an outstanding prospect as a friend.

So please,
when you see me grinning and acting fine,
behind my rosy glass of wine,
 search beyond the façade,
  step around my perfect presentation,
   and meet me in the garden of my vulnerability.
Maybe I'll discover that
you are lonely and needy too?

Guilt One

The Guilty ones say:
I'm bad.
I'm a terrible person.
I've screwed everything up.
I've ruined it for everyone.

Their litany goes on and on.

All their depreciatory comments
All their criticisms

All   beginning   with   "I"
I
I
I
I

I grow weary of the conceit of the Guilty.
Incessant crows cawing about themselves.

It is always their fault,
their error,
their mistake.

They have no time to consider laughter and smiles
— they are searching for frowns and disapproval.
They can't waste time sharing happiness
— they are too busy searching for what
THEY have done wrong.

I feel rotten for judging the Guilty so harshly.
I'm sure they don't enjoy their self-centered misery.
I tell myself, "*I should feel more compassion.*
I'm an insensitive jerk.
I am such an awful person!"

Then a hummingbird darts across my vision.
It zips back and hovers, pointing its bill between my eyes,
and I am out of the guilt prison.

I thank my friend as it dashes off in search of nectar.
Then I reach out to the guilty ones
          saying, "Join me. The flowers are open,
             and in their many-colored swirl
                judgments will blur
                   shifting I to us and guilt to joy."

GUILT TOO

I can't live with you in the Guilt House anymore.

I know you want me to contribute to your self-loathing,
  by being nice to you
  so you can feel unworthy.

But I just can't do it.

You see, I don't live in the Guilt House anymore.

Oh, I used to —
I knew all the closets marked "shame,"
the bedroom where I was bad,
the stains on the carpets I caused,
the meals that were never good enough,
served on the wrong plate,
eaten with the incorrect fork,
in the imperfect dining room.

I know the house that has no windows.
Only mirrors, to reflect back one's own inadequacies.
The house that has no mailbox outside — no need to solicit input from others,
when their opinions have already been decided for them.

I never could find the door out of that place —
So finally, in desperation, once I started hating the house,
instead of myself,
I burned the whole place down, using myself to fuel the fire.

Once the flames disappeared, I discovered I was standing in a meadow of wildflowers.
The sky was softly misting, crying all the silent tears
I could never release inside that prison.
Each glistening drop landing on a petal,
reflecting the rainbow arcing through the sky.

Yes, I know you still live in the Guilt House,
        but I am not there anymore.

Share Who You Are

Share who you are.
And I will listen.

By my listening
maybe you will hear yourself,
and explore.

And if we are really lucky
Maybe we will not find any answers.

Maybe
more and more
paths will open
to more and more
possibilities
of Being.

I Love You
Because

I do not love you
       because of what you have
done for me in the past.

I do not love you
       for what you will do for me
in the future.

I do not belittle who you are and what you do
       but that does not dictate my love.

I am the one who must enhance my love:
        water it with tears so it will grow,
        stretch it with courage so it will improve,
        nourish it with honesty so it will endure.

You, who are my love, do not determine my love.

I
   love
     you
       because
         I
          LOVE
            to
             love.

V
ADVENTURE

Don't Hit the Tree

From the top of the hill, all I see are wooden monoliths

guarding a narrow passageway.

My skis start to slip down the polished slope,

as I begin my chant: "Don't hit the tree."

"Don't hit the tree!"

Yards of clear snow speed by as I approach the first obstacle:

jagged bark and deadly broken branches

fringed with razor-sharp needles.

"Don't hit the tree."

"Don't hit the tree!"

WHAM!

I pull myself off the monster and try again.

Instructing myself, more forcefully.

"Don't hit the tree."

"Don't hit the tree!"

WHAM!

A skier glides over, untangling me from

the massive barrier.

"Are you okay? You skied straight into that tree."

I glare at him, then go back to muttering loudly,

 "Don't hit the tree. Don't hit the tree!"

He taps me on my shoulder.

"If you don't want to hit a tree, focus on the openings.

Here, I'll show you."

I watch as his skis turn toward a gap in

the surrounding fortress.

They soar through, then swerve toward

another gateway.

Soon he is halfway down the slope.

Crazy man, I think.

But I let my chant alter.

"Here's an opening."

"Here's an opening."

My skis start to glide on the fresh powder.

An opening appears between the trees,

my body turns and my skis match my thoughts.

"Here's an opening."

"Here's an opening."

The snow-sparkled forest offers me another opportunity.

Another opening, and another as the silent sentinels mark my path, encourage my journey.

"Here's an opening."

"Here's an opening."

BEYOND EXPECTATIONS

What if I sailed beyond expectations and fears?
    Kept going into the unknown
        beyond the bounds of predictability
           over the edge of — what?

What is beyond the lessons of society?
Beyond all the rules that teach us to worry about what
others think.

If I sailed beyond the edge of polite society, would I fall off?
      — into what? — selfishness and conceit — aloneness
        — would I be rejected or envied and would I care?

Self – ish – ness is all about the self. Well, is that so bad?
    To be about me?
        No one else can do it.

And if I am really, truly about me
    then I wouldn't need others to be about me.
        They could be about them.

So what if I did sail beyond expectations
    with no one watching
        and me not watching if others are watching.

      Where would I land?

Returning

Twenty years have passed and I walk down the exact same steps.
La Motte Picquet was my entrance to the underworld,
that fantastic web that connects all of Paris,
so blandly called 'le Metro.'

The stairs are the same dirty gray
with a tiny groove along the back and down the side of every step,
waiting to catch discarded tickets, to hold them for the night workers
and their sprays of water to wash them clean.

I insert my slim yellow passport at the turnstile.
I am allowed to pass — this far.
Signs point the way to the end of the lines,
Pont D'Orleans, Pont de la Chapelle,
I read each one — images of their journeys slowly filling my mind.
I follow the tunnels pointing toward Charenton Ecoles,
leading to the heart of the metropolis.

As I descend the final staircase I smell the platform,
waiting sweat mixed with day-old wine.
A small draft begins in this place below the winds.
A train is approaching, gliding in, no more screeching metal on metal.
Now the wheels roll smooth, almost quietly.

All the rest seems the same. I take the jump seat near the doors.
My stop arrives and the seat forgets me as soon as I stand up.
Exiting down the corridors I notice the second change.
Where are the guitar players with their cases awaiting a few francs?
Where are the immigrant women with children hoping for our spare metal?
If they are not allowed here — am I?

I ascend the last stairs, raising my head out from the depths.
I flow with the crowd down Boulevard Saint-Michel,
wander past the boulangerie, patisserie, and creamery.
At the corner is a sidewalk café,
there is one vacant table right in front.

The waitress offers me a menu, but I ignore it.
"Un croque-monsieur, s'il vous plait," I tell her.
"Tres bien," she says, smiling.

After she leaves I breathe in the aroma of coffee and baguettes, awaiting my meal.
Yes, Paris has awaited my return and it is still mine.

VI
SELF-REFLECTIONS

JAGGED JUDGMENTS

I throw stones,
  at myself.
"Idiot!" "Stupid." "Ugly."
"I can't do anything right."

I hurl the judgments one by one,
piling them up
until they rise, towering above me.

Weaving through columns of criticisms,
I worry over every word I utter,
"Will I sound stupid?" "Will I upset anyone?"
"Is it the right thing to say?"

I agonize for hours on the proper course to take,
as I navigate through the mounds of disapproval.
Always making sure the mountains are
invisible to everyone else.
- After all, I must be seen as positive,
- friendly,
- helpful.

People say nice things, which I try not to hear.
After all, polite people never appreciate themselves.
"Don't be conceited." "Selfish."
"No one likes a show-off."

I pick up a stone and throw one more
 "I'm worthless" at myself
and the rock walls shake.

Cascades of criticisms
tumble down the slopes
burying me.

Now I'm an absolute failure.
I can no longer even pretend for others.
They will see the mess I've made,
evidence of my inadequacy,
jumbled all around me.
So I hide.

But my dog discovers me.
He still wants his walks, his rubs, his food.
He strolls right through the piles of stony statements,
oblivious to the jagged judgments surrounding me.

My loveable Lab has never understood criticisms.
My scoldings never sink in.
He hangs his head — for a moment — then, wagging his tail,
he's back, expecting warmth and acceptance.

As I give love to him
his love for me sneaks in.
Tiny pebbles of pleasure
become a sandy beach.

Too tired to throw stones, I lie in the warmth
snuggling against my furry savior.

I agree with my earlier judgments.
I was an idiot
      — to worry so much.
I was stupid
      — to be so self-critical.
I'm going to start thinking — like my dog.

TOMORROW

I can't change tomorrow — today:
    — wrong time zone
    — wrong latitude
    — wrong attitude.

Every time I try to skip into the future
I end up right back where I am,
scrutinizing my crystal ball,
watching the images twist and spin,
certain each time
I can jump into next week,
and control something,
anything.
But I always land back in the present.

And I forget yesterdays
because I was never aware of today,
always chasing tomorrow.

ONE BITE

I maneuver my fork,
     positioning it precisely over the piece.
Holding it steady, I cut it with my knife.
     One measured bite — ready.
Spearing it with my fork,
     I raise it toward my mouth
and pause.

I'm still chewing.

Why am I reaching for more?

One bite in my mouth,
     one bite on my fork,
          where am I?

A half-chewed life.

Always reaching for what I already have.

TWO BITES

My plate is almost empty,
the food has disappeared.
Only two bites left.

I'd dreamed about the flavors,
anticipating the aromas,
desiring the taste.

And then,
I missed it.

Just two bites left.
I'll have to take a second piece now.
Not enough left to be satisfied.

I look again.
Two bites left.

I put down the paper,
turn off the television,
mute the phone,
and pause.

Two complete bites left.
Slowly, I take one of them into my mouth.
Resting on my tongue,
it begins to release its delicacies.
My mouth is a cavern
with a symphony of flavors vibrating
off the roof and harmonizing
on my taste buds.

Half the bite slides down my throat,
filling my chest with sensations of pleasure.
My belly tingles as the new atoms expand,
becoming the next step in my life,
becoming me.

I am still savoring that bite.
Taste buds overawed with impressions, passions.
I hold on, I don't give up
as my tongue floats across the cavern,
encircling lost flavors and
enticing them to release their fervor.

I need no second piece now.
I still have one more bite.

FAILURE

No. I didn't fail. Not me.

No one can say I failed,
because
I never said I would try.

I didn't fail on the job,
in the relationship,
with the project,
on the diet.

No. Not me.
I didn't try,
so I'm safe.

"*Happy?*" you ask.
No, not particularly.

But safe, and not a failure.

 "*What about Exploring and Learning?*" you ask.

Will they assure me of success?
Or give me the promise of perfection?

"*No*," you whisper, "*they have something else.*
Hope."

You want me to throw away the score card?
Mark the meaning of my days in values, not victories?
Risk defeat and devastation for hope and happiness?

Maybe.
    Maybe I will try.

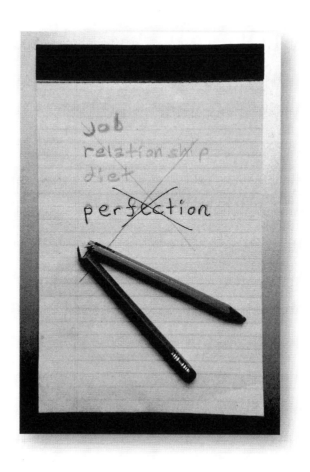

Energy

Energy knocked on my door.
A tall, vibrant woman in a long, blue, sequined dress.
"About time you showed up," I said, grabbing her hand and pulling
her into the house.
"There is so much to do. Let's start with the kitchen."
I didn't accomplish half of my list before she vanished.
I collapsed on the sofa.

Two days later Energy knocked on my door again.
A slim, athletic man in biking shorts and a shirt.
"There you are," I yelled, "just in time. I have to get the paperwork
done right away.
We can wash the laundry while we pay the bills."
He disappeared before the third load was folded.
I collapsed into the desk chair.

Five days later Energy knocked on my door again.
A spirited girl, in jeans and a tank top.
"Where have you been?" I demanded. "You can't just go off whenever you feel like
it. We have work to do. Come on." I led her into the dining room. "Company's
coming tonight and everything has to be just right."
"How much really needs to be done?" she asked forlornly.
"Not everything," I relented. "Promise not to leave and I'll make sure we take
some breaks."

Things were going so great that when my work called and asked if I could come by for a few minutes, I agreed.

"Energy," I called out, "since you're here I decided to stop by the office and maybe run a few errands. I'll be back soon."

When I returned, five hours later, Energy wasn't there to help me unload the car. I collapsed in the driver's seat.

It was a whole week before Energy knocked on my door again.

A lively boy carrying a baseball and two mitts.

"Want to play?" he asked.

"I should stay and get things done," I told him, leaning against the door frame.

"Ahhh, please. Just for a little while. Then I'll help you out," he offered.

"All right. If you promise."

We ran and tossed the ball and played tag.

We skipped back into the house together and cleaned both bathrooms before we stopped to think about it.

"Okay, now let's play basketball," he announced.

"No way. We're doing great. Let's keep going and see how much we can get done in here," I replied, starting to pull the vacuum out of the closet.

When I turned around, he was gone.

I walked outside, but I couldn't find him anywhere. I did discover there were tiny pink buds on the azalea bushes I hadn't managed to repot this winter.

Two weeks went by and I heard a knock on the door.

Energy was there.

The tall vibrant woman in the long, blue, sequined dress.

"Please come in," I said holding the door open for her. "Have a seat."

I served her some tea, then sat down next to her.

"What do you want to do?" I asked.

She smiled. "Shall we drink our tea?"

Sipping, chatting and laughing, we became friends.

When we finished the tea, she rose and held out her hand.

"Shall we go do a few things?" she offered.

"Gladly," I responded, taking her hand and standing up.

As I started to pull out my list, I stopped and turned to her.

"You lead," I suggested.

We've been dancing together ever since.